THE
EAST END
AT WAR

Children pictured in 1919, laying flowers at the memorial in Poplar Recreation Ground to the eighteen children who were killed at Upper North Street School on 13 June 1917.

THE
EAST END
AT WAR

ROSEMARY TAYLOR AND
CHRISTOPHER LLOYD

SUTTON PUBLISHING

This book was first published in 2000 by Sutton Publishing Limited

This new paperback edition first published in 2007 by
Sutton Publishing, an imprint of NPI Media Group
Cirencester Road · Chalford · Stroud · Gloucestershire · GL6 8PE

British Library Cataloguing in Publication Data
A catalogue record for this book is available from the British Library.

ISBN 978-0-7509-4913-2

Front endpaper: Recruitment bus outside the Army Recruitment Office, East India Dock Road, Poplar, shortly after war had been declared between Britain and Germany, on Tuesday 4 August 1914. The bus ran from the Tower of London to Poplar, with its destination board displaying: 'To Berlin and Back Free'. This was a reference to advertisements inviting day trippers to take an August Bank Holiday train and boat trip to Boulogne at 11s 6d return, with a trip to Calais costing a bit more.

Back endpaper: The Garden of Remembrance in Tower Hamlets Cemetery, Bow. Laid out in 1952 to commemorate the burial of 190 people who lost their lives in Poplar during the first six months of the Blitz and who were buried in five common graves on the site. Following the takeover of the cemetery in 1969, the GLC removed all traces of the garden when a road was created to enable vehicles to drive around the cemetery. All that remains is the wall and the plaque, with no reference points to the sites of the common graves.

Half title page: Painting, *Red Sunday*, 1940, by W.S. Haines, from *PLA Monthly*, May 1942. Wilfred Haines was the official artist of the London Fire Force, River Command, and was on duty afloat during the Blitz.

Title page: Aerial photograph taken by the Germans of a Heinkel 111, 7 September 1940. This picture was discovered in the German archives in 1945, and shows the aircraft over the Surrey Commercial Docks crossing the Thames to the west of the loop of the Isle of Dogs. The West India and Millwall Docks, the East India Dock Road and Commercial Road are all clearly identifiable. Although the sugar and other warehouses were severely damaged and the docks burned furiously for days, they continued to operate. Few of the rows of tightly packed terraced houses escaped damage or destruction in the Blitzkrieg, and the V1 and V2 rocket attacks that followed.

Typeset in 11/14pt Photina.
Typesetting and origination by
Sutton Publishing.
Printed and bound in England.

Contents

View of the inside of an air raid shelter, 1940. The claustrophobic atmosphere this view conjures up reflects the authorities' concerns that sending people into these shelters would create a condition described as 'deep shelter mentality'. The theory was that once down below ground, people would remain there, too afraid to come up again.

Introduction

The year 2000 marks the 60th anniversary of the onset of the London Blitz when the three Metropolitan Boroughs of Stepney, Bethnal Green and Poplar bore the brunt of the German bombardment which began in earnest that fateful day, 7 September 1940. When William Joyce, 'Lord Haw-Haw', made his broadcast warning of Germany's intention to bomb London and Londoners, he stated, 'Hardest of all, the Luftwaffe will smash Stepney'. Stepney knew Joyce well, he was one of Mosley's men, defeated in local elections and treated with contempt. Nobody could believe a word he said – until it happened.

Unfortunately, the strategic importance of the docks in the East End of London was only too well known to the Germans. Enemy bombing during the Second World War had a devastating effect on the area, destroying thousands of homes, factories, shops and businesses. The total number of civilians killed by enemy action in the London area numbered 19,000. In Tower Hamlets alone, 2,221 people were killed and 7,472 injured; in some cases whole families were wiped out in an instant. The destruction to property was immense – 46,482 houses were destroyed, 47,574 damaged.

The photographs in our main selection are a graphic reminder of those dark days, when it seemed the bombing would never end: from the build-up to the conflict, the trench-digging and sandbagging, the evacuation of children, the destruction caused by the enemy, and the heroism of the people who fought to hold on to what they had. But they also illustrate the indomitable Cockney spirit, the stoicism of the people of the East End, who carried on regardless, and finally, when it was all over, the celebrations and finally the gradual rebuilding of their lives, their homes and their community. Stories of great heroism and personal sacrifice have come to light over the years, and unfortunately, there is sufficient space here to recount but a few.

Group of Volunteers performing the command 'pile arms'. Left, Mile End Volunteer, centre, Shoreditch Volunteer, right, Trinity Minories Volunteer. The Mile End Volunteers were originally Bethnal Green Volunteers.

7

Where the East End begins and ends has always been a matter of discussion and contention, and in order to simplify our research we have confined our work to the area now known as Tower Hamlets, using the Thames and the Lea as natural boundaries to the south and east, Victoria Park to the north, and Bishopsgate to the west.

The East End of London has for centuries influenced the City of London, which appreciated the strategic importance of the area east of the Tower of London. With the building of the Tower by William the Conqueror, the Constable of the Tower looked to the hamlets along the north bank of the Thames for its supply of yeomen to guard it. We have evidence of the existence of Trained Bands in the East End from a muster which took place during the reign of Charles I on 26 September 1643. The Tower Hamlets Regiment consisted of 849 muskets, 385 pikes and 70 officers, a total of 1,304 with 7 ensigns or colours.

In 1794 the Trained Bands were reorganised as Volunteers, and at the review of the Volunteer and Associated Corps held in Hyde Park on 4 June 1799, the following Tower Hamlets regiments attended: Mile End, Whitechapel, Ratcliff, Limehouse, Blackwall and Poplar, Bromley, Shoreditch, Hackney, Wapping and Christchurch. These Volunteer Militia Companies were held in readiness against the threat of an invasion by Napoleon. As the name indicates, these men were not forced into compulsory military service, as was the case during the First World War, when conscription began. When the threat of invasion from the continent receded, the importance of the volunteer militia companies declined.

The creation and expansion of the British Empire, which led to the rapid increase in trade with every corner of the world, gradually caused chaotic operating conditions in the Port of London. Ships from the West Indies, the East Indies and China arrived at London with their precious cargoes of spices, sugar, rum, ivory, tobacco and tea, and often had to wait for weeks if not months to offload their goods. Large-scale theft and looting became almost a way of life on the river. In 1793, soon after France had declared war on England, some concerned West India merchants formed a committee to agitate for dock reforms, and the wartime conditions accelerated the plans to replace the legal quays system with a more secure and more efficient dock system. The East India and the West India Docks, the London Docks and St Katharine's, were constructed along the River Thames. This inevitably resulted in a rapid increase in population in the East End of London as the docks attracted a large labour force, first to

A naval airship of the Beta type cruising over Cotton Street, at the junction with East India Dock Road. Although this picture is dated precisely as Wednesday 20 October 1915, this is now open to question.

build them and then to assist with the daily loading and unloading of vessels, and storing imported goods in the vast warehouses alongside the quays. But while there was work to be had in the docks and in the factories and sweatshops which proliferated towards the end of the 19th century, thousands of families struggled for survival in vastly overcrowded slums and tenements.

The onset of the First World War only added to the misery of women and children left behind to fend for themselves with their menfolk at the battlefront, and the East End had its share of bombardment, first by night from the Zeppelins, when the area was bombed indiscriminately, leading to the deaths of innocent civilians.

Then, on 13 June 1917, the first daylight aerial bombing of civilians by fixed-wing aircraft targeted London. Fourteen Gothas, led by Squadron Commander, Hauptmann Ernst Brandenberg, flew over Essex, and began dropping their bombs. Liverpool Street Station, Fenchurch Street, Aldgate and Hoxton were all hit by high explosive (HE) bombs. In the East End alone, 104 were killed, 154 seriously injured and 269 slightly injured. Among the casualties were 120 children, killed and injured. One HE bomb destroyed a school in Poplar and killed 18 children, injuring many more, although the exact number was never recorded. The full horror of the war was brought home to the people of the East End. There was an

Poplar Borough Council workmen constructing a temporary air raid shelter in Judkin Street, on the Isle of Dogs, September 1939. The little street, just off East Ferry Road, was in the vicinity of the docks.

outpouring of grief, both locally and nationally, and a memorial to the children was erected in Poplar Recreation Park.

The end of the war saw the slow return to normality for some families, as those men who returned tried to adjust to civilian life. Peace parties were organised in streets all over the East End, as people celebrated what they believed would be the beginning of an era of lasting peace and harmony the world over.

But the East End remained scarred and bruised by its experiences of war for decades to come. Twenty years later, with the renewed outbreak of hostilities, the enemy once again brought the war into their homes.

The build-up to the Second World War saw preparations in the East End with trench-digging in the parks and the sandbagging of strategic buildings such as the town halls. The evacuation of thousands of women and children to the countryside, the introduction of Air Raid Precautions and the 'black-out' brought home the gravity of the situation. From September 1939 the East End stood in readiness for attacks from the air and, as the months went by, some actually came to believe they would never happen.

But the war came closer to home in August 1940 with German air raids on RAF airfields close to London. Also under attack were the oil storage tanks at Purfleet and Thames Haven. All these targets were within the London Defence Region and as the air raid sirens in London sounded everything in the capital came to a halt, all traffic stopped, all work stopped. Everyone went to the bomb shelters and fire services; civil defence units and hospitals went on full alert until the 'All Clear' was given. These constant air raid warnings disrupted the normal pattern of sleep and work. The strict censorship in force prevented the press and radio disseminating news of the desperate air battles that were taking place over Kent, so few people were aware of them.

Civil Defence Search and Rescue team in action during the Blitz. These men worked with little thought for their own safety; their main concern was to rescue victims who were trapped under the rubble of their homes. Casualties among the Civil Defence staff were high in the East End.

All that changed on Saturday 24 August at 3 pm. Four groups of bombers attacked the airfields at Hornchurch and North Weald. Five bombers were shot down at Hornchurch but North Weald received heavy damage and was out of action for a time. A few stray bombs fell on Dagenham and Upminster, the closest the action came to East London.

That night the bombers returned, and the first air raid on central London since 1918 took place. At some time between 11.30 pm and 1.30 am a bomb fell on Tower Hamlets Cemetery. There were no reported deaths or injuries but houses in nearby streets had their windows blown out. Tower Hamlets Cemetery was not the only place to be bombed that night. Stepney, Bethnal Green, East Ham, West Ham, Edmonton, Walthamstow and the City all got their share of bombs.

Winston Churchill's response to the bombing of London was to order retaliatory raids on Berlin, and although the RAF raids did very little damage, with no casualties, the psychological impact was enormous. Adolf Hitler stated that for every bomb on Germany the British would receive ten German bombs, and so it all started.

On Saturday 7 September 1940, the Luftwaffe targeted London and the East End bore the brunt of the attacks. The docks were set ablaze and the East End endured months of continuous bombardment. The destruction of whole streets, reduced to rubble, has often been referred to as 'Hitler's slum clearance'. Evacuation of women and children disrupted and fragmented family life, and returning evacuees often found their homes had been completely obliterated. An amazing story was published by the London *Evening Standard* of 'Amy Gray', an orphan befriended by a gang of East End absconded evacuee children, about twenty of whom survived during the war, sleeping in cellars by day and foraging for food and firewood at dawn. Other stories of heroism and fortitude are too numerous to be related here, and our account is limited to the photographic evidence available. Inevitably, some great tragedies, such as the bombing of Bullivant's Shelter on the Isle of Dogs, which saw a great loss of life, and details of the destruction in the docks and warehouses have been omitted for this reason.

Map of Stepney showing the locations of all incidents which occurred between 1939 and 1945. Heavy explosives, landmines, V1 and V2 rocket explosions are all marked, but incendiaries have been excluded.

11

Innumerable tragedies were enacted all over the East End during the first months of the Blitz, when the enemy barely allowed the emergency services to rescue the living and give the dead a decent burial. Those who had surviving family members who could afford to make funeral arrangements were claimed for private burial, and there are rows of wartime graves in Tower Hamlets Cemetery. Others unclaimed or unidentified were buried in mass graves, the funeral being paid for by the local council.

Tower Hamlets Cemetery has two mass graves containing 169 bodies which were identified, and 71 bodies which were unidentified (including 'pieces'). Many unidentified and unclaimed bodies from Stepney were interred in a common grave in Manor Park Cemetery. Bethnal Green's 23 unclaimed bodies were interred in a communal grave at the City of London Cemetery, Manor Park, as were the civilian war dead of Hackney whose names are recorded on a large slab, while those of West Ham are remembered in a memorial in the shape of a large cross with panels with the names of all those interred in a mass grave in the same cemetery.

Members of the Civil Defence Services such as Air Raid Wardens, Heavy Rescue Service, Ambulance Crews and Fire Brigade Personnel who were killed on duty were buried in individual graves with headstones provided by the Commonwealth War Graves Commission. Some of these can be found in the City of London Manor Park Cemetery, Military Plot.

The end of the war in Europe was greeted with the wildest of celebrations, and parties and parades were organised with great enthusiasm. With the surrender of Japan, the terrible war was finally over, and it was time to take stock of the destruction and damage, and the slow return to normality began.

A great deal of postwar rebuilding took place under the aegis of the newly formed Greater London Council and, as the pace of rebuilding accelerated, tower blocks began to make an appearance on the landscape. Postwar reconstruction altered the landscape, in some cases obliterating streets and familiar landmarks. The regeneration of the docklands and the construction of the Canary Wharf complex has transformed the Isle of Dogs from being the hub of London's import and export trade and industry into what is rapidly becoming London's financial centre. Rebuilding and construction work continues in Tower Hamlets to the present day, and from time to time unexploded bombs are discovered on building sites, the most recent one being in Harford Street, Mile End, on 3 August 1998. This was safely detonated by the Army Bomb Squad the following day.

The Harford Street incident, August 1998. The army bomb squad was called in to defuse an unexploded 50 kg bomb found by builders during excavations in Harford Street, Stepney. On the right the detonated bomb leaves a wisp of smoke. In the centre of the picture is the spire of St Anne's Church, Limehouse, while in the distance the Canary Wharf complex in docklands has replaced the wharves and warehouses of West India Docks, which suffered tremendous damage and destruction during the Blitz.

Past Centuries

LAUNCH OF A WAR-STEAMER AT LIMEHOUSE DOCKYARD.

1855

Launch of war steamer *Victoria* at Limehouse Dockyard, from the *Illustrated London News* dated 7 July 1855. Cox and Curling of Limehouse, later known as Curling and Young or Young and Magnay, was just north of the entrance to the West India Dock basin. These were among the last of the shipyards to continue building sailing ships when other yards were building steamships.

Drawing captioned 'An exact representation of the shooting of the three Highlanders on the Parade in the Tower. July 19 1743.' A rebellion by discontented Highland soldiers in the King's service resulted in their capture and execution at the Tower of London. The three men are, from right to left, Samuel McPherson, shot in the ear after he was down, Malcolm McPherson, shot dead the first shot, and Farquhar Shaw, shot in the forehead after he was down. The two gentlemen standing left are the Rev. Pattison and Campbell, and on the right Sergeant Major Ellison who gave the signal with his handkerchief. The execution party consisted of twelve Scots guards and six more standing by. Surrounding the men are one hundred Highland prisoners forced to witness the event, and 300 Scots Guards in three lines. During both the First and Second World Wars several German spies were executed at the Tower, among them Fernando Buschman on 19 October 1915 and Josef Jakobs on 15 August 1941.

Ratcliff Volunteer, 21 September 1798. The 'Make Ready' command, when the firelock is brought to the same position as 'Recover' at the same time cocking it. From a series of paintings by D. Rowlanson.

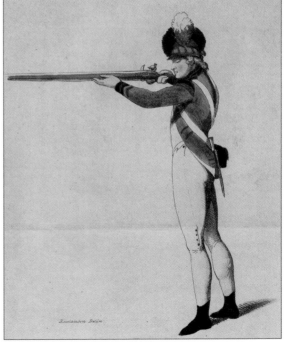

Union Wapping Volunteer, 24 September 1798. The Corps was formed on 27 April of that year, under the command of Peter Mellish, with the aim of protecting 'Our Liberties and Properties, also to defend our invaluable Constitution under which we live, from all the attacks of its avowed and secret enemies; and in the case of invasion, be ready to assist in protecting the following parishes viz., St John's Wapping, St George's Middlesex and St Paul's Shadwell.' One of a series of paintings by D. Rowlanson.

Poplar and Blackwall Volunteer, at the command 'Prime and Load', from a series of paintings by D. Rowlanson, dated 21 September 1798.

Bethnal Green Battalion, Volunteer, at the command 'Support Arms, 2nd Motion', dated 16 June 1798. The Corps was first formed under John Liptrap in May 1793 and consisted of two companies of about sixty rank and file, which were affiliated to Wapping and Whitechapel. They later became the Mile End Volunteers. From a series of paintings by D. Rowlanson.

Army of Defence

HAMLET of RATCLIFF.

Wanted,

THIRTY-THREE MEN

FOR THIS HAMLET,

TO enlist as VOLUNTEERS under the Act of Parliament of the 44th Geo. III. Ch. 56, for establishing and maintaining a permanent additional Force for the Defence of the Realm, and to provide for augmenting His Majesty Regular Forces, and for the gradual Reduction of the Militia of England, to whom fuch Bounties will be given as are allowed according to His Majesty's Regulations in that Behalf.

For further Particulars apply to the Churchwardens and Overfeers of the Poor of the faid Hamlet, or to

J. BARNFIELD, *Vestry-Clerk,*

No. 82, BROAD-STREET, RATCLIFF.

MARCH 28, 1805.

Recruitment poster issued by the vestry clerk, J. Barnfield, for the Hamlet of Ratcliff, 28 March 1805. 'Wanted, Thirty-Three Men for this Hamlet, to enlist as volunteers, under the Act of Parliament . . . for the Defence of the Realm.'

Ensign 2nd Tower Hamlets Volunteers, *c.* 1865. Until 1871 the title of ensign was given to officers of the lowest commissioned rank in the British infantry.

2nd Tower Hamlets Rifle Volunteer group, 1900. The Tower Hamlets Rifle Volunteer Brigade was formed in 1874, from an amalgamation of local volunteer corps. Several officers and men of the brigade were awarded campaign medals in the Crimea, South Africa, India and Egypt. It became the Fourth Volunteer Battalion, the Royal Fusiliers, City of London Regiment, in 1903, until the creation of the Territorial Army in 1908. The TA headquarters are in Mile End Road.

One of the twenty-three torpedo boats built for the government by Messrs Yarrow and Co. The boat has the words 'official trial 11 March 1886' painted on the hull. Her length was 125 ft, and beam 13 ft. In 1875 Yarrow and Headley fitted one of their launches with a spar torpedo and in 1876 they sold their first torpedo boat to a foreign navy, probably Argentina. Torpedo boats were built for Argentina, Spain, France, Holland, Greece, Austria, Russia, Italy and Chile as well as the Royal Navy. In the 1880s there was no requirement for shipbuilders to inform the Admiralty, the Foreign Office or anyone else about the warships they built for foreign navies.

Torpedo boat No. 80, the fastest vessel in Her Majesty's Navy, built by Yarrow and Co. at their shipyard on the Isle of Dogs, March 1887. With a length of 135 ft, and beam of 14 ft. she was capable of a speed of 23 knots for a two-hour run, carrying 15 tons.

Baron Kato, Japanese minister, inspecting the progress of the battleship *Fuji* under construction for his
country at the Thames Ironworks, Blackwall, on 18 March 1895. The Thames Ironworks had its slipways on
the Blackwall side of the River Lea and the workshops and stores on the West Ham side with a floating bridge
in between. The firm made its own angles, plates and armour-plate. The shipbuilding firm was started by C.J.
Mare, who went bankrupt in 1856. It was then taken over by a board of directors. In 1880 Arnold Hills joined
the company and the Thames Ironworks prospered for the next thirty years.

Imperial Japanese battleship *Fuji*, built for the Japanese Navy in 1894. She had a length of 374 ft and breadth of 73 ft and a speed of 18.5 knots. The vessel was an improvement on the Admiral class of the British Navy, having an additional deck forward and aft of the citadel, giving 8 ft more height of freeboard, which prevented the sea coming over the deck and provided excellent quarters for the crew and officers. The ship was designed for service near home and not to carry the Imperial flag to distant parts of the globe.

IJB *Shikishima*, 1897. Length 400 ft, breadth 75.5 ft, speed 18 knots. The Japanese government ordered this ship to be built at Thames Ironworks, following the success of the *Fuji*. At the close of the Russo-Japanese war, after heavy fighting during which the Russian fleet was wiped out, only two Japanese battleships were stilll serviceable – the *Fuji* and the *Shikishima*.

The armour-clad *Vasco Da Gama*, built at the Thames Ironworks in 1878 for the Portuguese government. Length 200 ft, breadth 40 ft and speed 13.5 knots. She was armed with two 26 cm guns, one 15 cm gun, and two machine guns. The picture shows the vessel after reconstruction in 1901.

Prussian government armour-clad *Konig Wilhelm* built at the Thames Ironworks in 1867. The vessel had a length of 355 ft, a breadth of 60 ft and could reach a speed of 14.7 knots. She had eighteen 24 cm BLR guns, five 21 cm guns, six 15 cm guns and machine guns.

George Green School Cadet Corps NCOs, *c.* 1911. Second from right, front row, is Francis James White, aged about fourteen years. He later joined the 6th Battalion Essex Regiment, and was killed on 27 March 1917 in the Palestine Campaign at Gaza.

Poplar National Reserve leaving St Luke's Church, Millwall, Isle of Dogs, after Church Parade on Sunday 14 September 1913.

The Poplar Battalion, National Reserve, first Church Parade held on 20 October 1912. The battalion is marching down East India Dock Road, past George Green's School and the Recreation Tavern, which was on the corner of Kerbey Street, heading towards the East India Dock gates.

General Alfred Gaselee inspecting the Reservists in Poplar Recreation Ground during the first Church Parade, 20 October 1912. The veteran general led his troops into battle on the North West Frontier in 1897. He was the Commander of the 20,000 strong International Relief of Peking Expedition, and succeeding in rescuing the Europeans held captive during the Boxer Rebellion on 14 August 1900.

The First World War

Isaac Rosenberg, Stepney poet and painter, with his brother Elkon standing beside him, is pictured while home on leave in September 1917. Isaac Rosenberg's talents were first recognised by his headmaster at the Baker Street School in Stepney and encouraged by the librarian in Whitechapel Library. He joined the army in October 1915 and was killed in action on 1 April 1918.

Anti-German riots in High Street, Poplar, 1915. According to Sylvia Pankhurst in *The Home Front* these raids on German shops and property were organised by men unknown in the East End, who came along with their hatchets to break down the shutters and the glass, following which crowds of children would rush in and loot the shop. The police all too often made little or no attempt to intervene or arrest the perpetrators.

This scene occurred during the riots and looting following the sinking of the *Lusitania*, 1915. German shops in Chrisp Street are being attacked. No. 186 was A. Schoenfelds, next door to P. Appleton. Shortly after this picture was taken the shop was wrecked and goods and even furniture was carried away, including a harmonium, which was passed down to the crowd from an upstairs window. Two policemen stand by the shop while two others attempt to control the crowd, with no visible effect.

No. 130 St Leonard's Street damaged by a bomb dropped from a Zeppelin shortly after midnight on 24 September 1916. One 100 kg HE and five incendiary bombs fell first in St Leonard's Street and Empson Street, Bow, wrecking four two-storeyed houses and breaking windows in a large number of others. Six people were killed and eleven injured here. The bomb which fell in St Leonard's Street hit W. Lusty's timber yard. It also practically wiped out a row of small houses and among those killed were George Scott Jones (41), Harry Brown (54), Harriet Diewett (53), and Mary Lumas (74). Blanche Bradford died later from her injuries and another 22 people were injured.

Damage to the rear of 746 Old Ford Road, Bow, from the Zeppelin raid at 12.15 am on 23 September 1916.
The L33 dropped a 100 kg HE bomb at the junction of Old Ford and Wrexham Road, injuring three women.
The L33 Zeppelin, commanded by Kapitanleutnant Aloysius Bocker, appeared over Wanstead where at 11.59
pm she suddenly turned south-east and at 12.06 turned south-west between the Beckton and North Woolwich
guns, afterwards turning again north-west towards West Ham where she passed over the gun at 12.10 am.
The airship was hit by a shell which pierced her hull and eventually Bocker brought her down in a field some
3 miles inland north-east of Mersea.

The Black Swan public house at the corner of Devons Road and Bow Road, Bromley by Bow, damaged by Zeppelin air raid on 23 September 1916. A 100 kg bomb smashed through the house, taking all the floors to the basement. The Reynolds family who had just gone upstairs to bed were all found lying in the cellar. Cissie Reynolds (19) and her sister Sylvia Adams were killed along with Sylvia's 13-month-old daughter, also Sylvia, who was found hanging by her clothes from the rafters, but died of shock later. Mrs Potter, the girls' grandmother, also died. George Reynolds (8) and his brother Sydney Reynolds (9) were injured, along with Henry Adams, Sylvia's husband. Harry Taylor (4) was also killed when the adjoining house was practically wrecked.

29

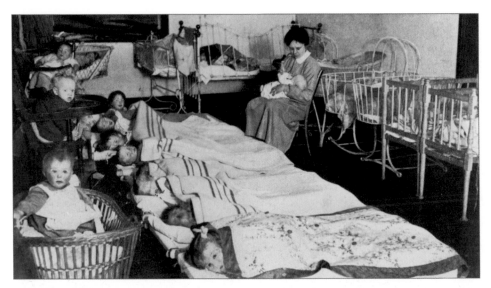

The Mothers Arms, Old Ford Road, Bow, 1915. Nurse Hebbes attends to the children at the mother and baby clinic. The Mothers Arms was set up by Sylvia Pankhurst in April 1915 in a disused pub at 438 Old Ford Road, on the corner of St Stephen's Road, in response to the growing hardship faced by families struggling to survive during the First World War, with little or no support from the government. The clinic was staffed by two doctors, Alice Johnson and Barbara Tchaykovsky, and nurse Maud Hebbes.

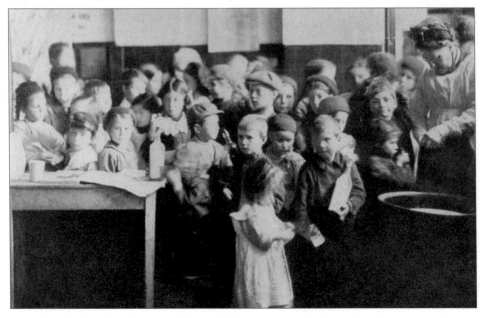

Distribution of milk at 20 Railway Street, Poplar, 1915. Formerly a public house, the premises were taken over by Sylvia Pankhurst for use as the Poplar headquarters of the East London Federation of the Suffragettes. Free milk and Virol (malt) were handed out to mothers with small children. The centre organiser was Mrs Schlette.

30

Commercial Gas Company Munitions Foundry, Stepney. *c.* 1915. As the need for munitions increased, so did the output from factories such as this one. Here the molten metal is poured into wooden cases, each half the size of a gun case.

Commercial Gas Company Munitions Foundry, *c.* 1915. As the war progressed more and more women workers were being recruited for munitions work. Here two young women are standing by a saw which they employed to cut up logs which were used for casting metal.

Issy Smith, awarded the VC for bravery at the Second Battle of Ypres, 26 April 1915. The first Jewish NCO to receive the award, Issy was born in Stepney in 1886 and was just 19 when he risked his life to save a colleague. Shortly after this he was gassed, and was hospitalised in Dublin. He was again injured in March 1917, when the boat he was on was torpedoed. Issy emigrated to Australia, where he died on 11 September 1940.

Private Sidney Godley, 4th Battalion Royal Fusiliers (City of London Regiment), who was awarded the VC on 23 August 1914 for coolness and gallantry in fighting, after he had been wounded at Mons. Godley was caretaker of Cranbrook Street School, Bethnal Green.

The Mayor of Poplar, Councillor A. Warren presents Mr A.W. Day, an ex-soldier of the Royal Fusiliers, with a donkey and cart, through the Lord Kitchener National Memorial Fund, to enable him to earn a living as a costermonger, 15 November 1916. The presentation took place outside the Poplar Town Hall in Newby Place.

Postcard dated 16 November 1915, captioned 'Wounded Tommies at the London Hospital'. A message on the back, probably written by one of the nurses, says: 'What do you think of our boys? They keep smiling in spite of their wounds.'

Wounded Belgian soldiers convalescing in Annie Zunz Ward at the London Hospital, Whitechapel, *c*. 1915. Nurse Edith Cavell, who trained and worked at the London Hospital, later moved to Belgium to continue her nursing career. She was shot by a German firing squad on 12 October 1915, having been accused of spying.

Drawing from the *Sphere* magazine showing the scene at the Upper North Street School, following the Gotha aircraft attack on 13 June 1917. The caption reads: 'The air attack on "The Fortress" of London – carrying some of the victims to the hospitals.' When the British government protested that Germany was targeting women and children, their reply was that they held the British government responsible, as the Germans regarded London as a fortress containing munitions works, military installations, and defended by heavy guns. They advised the British government to remove all civilians from London.

The scene shows firemen, policemen and ambulancemen, who were assisted by sailors and soldiers home on leave.

The upper floor of the school. To the left of the picture can be seen the hole in the ceiling of the boys' classroom, where the bomb entered, demolishing the floor, before continuing its journey down to the ground floor. Mrs Watkins, teacher in the Infants' class, reported that three big boys had fallen through the ceiling into her class below. Edwin Powell, aged 12, was killed. Frederick Pepper, aged 10, recalls that there was a terrible explosion and red dust everywhere, and where his schoolfriend had been sitting alongside him, there was only a large hole. Agnes Hill, then aged 14, remembers 'the horror of it, and the unbelief, it couldn't be, you know that class was there and then it wasn't'.

A workman searches through the debris in the bomb crater in the ground floor classroom following the bomb attack. One of the children, Rose Symmons, was rescued three days after the incident after her brother Jimmy, aged 12, refused to leave the school and continued searching for her. She was found alive though badly injured, and made a good recovery. Eighteen children died in the explosion: five died instantly from skull fractures, eleven children were pronounced dead on 14 June, their injuries being mainly fractured skulls and crush injuries, and two children were pronounced dead on 15 June. It took several days to extricate the bodies from the rubble in the classroom. Dr O'Brien reported that all the children in this classroom were covered with debris and could not be seen. Mrs Middleton, the teacher, although injured, stayed on the scene, pointing out places where children were likely to be found.

Funeral of the children killed at the Upper North Street School. The funeral procession passes along the East India Dock Road on 20 June 1917. Fifteen children were buried in a common grave in East London Cemetery, Plaistow, and a sixteenth coffin with unidentifed remains was also interred. Three children were buried

Alderman Sam March and Mrs March, Mayor and Mayoress, at the service of remembrance to the eighteen children who had died as a result of the bombing of Upper North Street School. This was held three years later, on 13 June 1920.

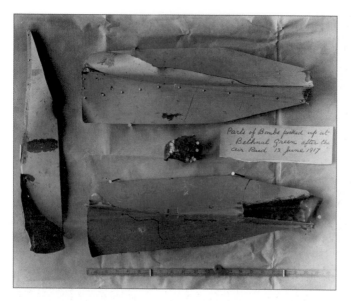

Parts of bombs picked up at Bethnal Green after the air raid of 13 June 1917. Rochelle Street was hit and six men, six women and ten children were injured. A bomb fell about 11.40 am at 18 Gibraltar Walk, Bethnal Green, killing two women and two children, and injuring 17 others. In the East End alone, 104 were killed, 154 seriously injured and 269 slightly injured. Among the casualties were 120 children, killed and injured. The Squadron Commander, Hauptmann Ernst Brandenberg, who led the Gotha attack, became a national hero in Germany, and was awarded the Blue Max for his good work in destroying a number of military targets. The next day, while returning to his base, Brandenberg crashed and was badly injured. He recovered and after the war went on to help found Lufthansa Airlines.

Nos 30 and 31 Charlotte Street, off Turin Street, Bethnal Green. One man was killed and a man and a woman injured at 30 Charlotte Street during the Gotha attack. The houses were the property of the family of Lord Kenyon. Several bombs fell in the area around Great Eastern Street, Curtain Road, Flower and Dean Street and Fashion Street.

Children at a Poplar Peace Party, 1919. The exact location is not known, but it is typical of the many street parties held all over the East End.

Celebrating the peace in Hall Street, Poplar, 1919. One of those celebrating here was Grace Gibson, standing to the right of the picture, wearing a sailor suit. She was twenty-two at the time and worked as a cutter and dryer in a tobacco manufacturers in Aldgate, earning 26s 6d per week.

Children's Peace Party in St Leonard's Road, Poplar, 1919.

Rev. W.H. Lax, Mayor of Poplar, with residents of a street in Poplar, during peace festivities, 1919. Rev. Lax was the Minister of the Methodist Church in the East India Dock Road. He was a flamboyant character, who through his lecture tours and books helped to raise awareness of the poverty and hardship that existed in the area. In his autobiography *Lax – His Book* he claims that he and his wife thought up the idea of 'Street Teas' so that Poplar's 41,000 children could all celebrate the armistice.

Lt Col. G E Holman unveiling the Bruce Provident Dividing Society's war memorial. Bruce Road Congregational Church, September 1919. The road is adjacent to St Leonard's Street, Bromley by Bow, where the first bomb was dropped from the Zeppelin on the night of 24 September 1916.

War Memorial in St Leonard's Road, Poplar. In the background is the vicarage of St Michael and All Angels. The memorial was unveiled on 4 December 1920.

The Rt Rev. the Bishop of Stepney unveils a war memorial at the Marner Street School, Bromley, 31 January 1923. Mr T.R. Rand, the headmaster, is on the extreme right. The memorial listed the names of 93 old Marner boys, who died in the First World War, which a local newspaper reported was 'a splendid record for one school'.

The Shadow of War

Home Guards March Past in Wilmot Street, Bethnal Green, 1939. From January 1939, men and women were encouraged to volunteer as Civil Defence personnel. In May 1940 Anthony Eden broadcast an appeal for people aged between forty and sixty-five to join as Local Defence Volunteers. From 23 July 1940 the name was changed to the Home Guard.

Demonstration against German Pogroms. This scene is outside a Jewish shop in Stepney. The *East London Advertiser* poster announcing the death of Mrs Lansbury, in the issue dated 25 March 1933, dates this picture accurately. A man has interrupted his shave to pose for the camera while the shopkeeper sets light to a paper bag which the poster proclaims to be a 'German Spy'. Stepney's large Jewish population was becoming increasingly alarmed by reports of Nazi atrocities on the German Jews, and meetings and demonstrations were held throughout the East End.

The Major Attlee Company banner displayed. In December 1937 Clement Attlee went briefly to Spain where he was photographed giving the clenched fist (anti-fascist) salute. The British Battalion of the International Brigade that had been formed on a volunteer basis to assist the Spanish Loyalists included a Clement Attlee Company.

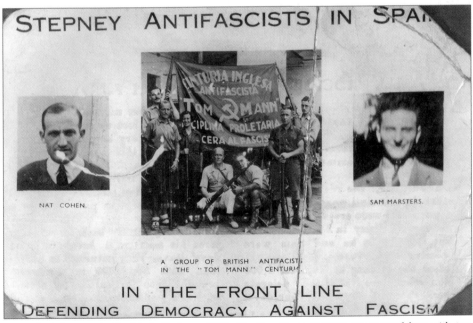

Postcard of Stepney Antifascists in Spain, c. 1936. The Tom Mann Centuria are pictured here with two members of the group, Nat Cohen and Sam Marsters.

The Duke of Kent inspects young cadets at the Prince of Wales Sea Training Hostel, Newell Street, Limehouse, 6 May 1938. The Duke, younger brother of King George VI, joined the RAF in 1939 and rose to the rank of Air Commodore. He was to die in a plane crash in the north of Scotland on 25 August 1942. The hostel for boys opened on 25 February 1920, with 21 boys, later increased to 48, who were trained for the Merchant Navy. The hostel was built and run by the British and Foreign Sailors' Society, whose headquarters was situated at the Passmore Edwards Sailors' Palace in Commercial Road, at the junction with West

Sea cadets line up for inspection by Commodore Sir Edgar Britten, Captain of the liner *Queen Mary*, who made a surprise visit to the Prince of Wales Sea Training Hostel in Limehouse, 1938. The cadets were selected to serve on British merchant ships after a training course which lasted six months, during which the boys were instructed in all aspects of seamanship and navigation. Orphans of sailors were given priority admission, and the British and Foreign Sailors Society kept in touch with the boys during their early days at sea.

At the Poplar Hippodrome, East India Dock Road, an appeal for volunteers for Civil Defence services is launched in April 1939. Voluntary Civil Defence work was eventually made compulsory in 1943, and subject to fines from £2 to 50 guineas or imprisonment for those who refused to 'volunteer'.

Councillor Mrs E.M. Lambert, Mayor of Poplar, opening the first ARP training class held in the borough, Monday 25 April 1938, at the Council offices, Poplar. On her right is the Town Clerk, H.E. Dennis. Corps Supt A.A. Smith of the St John Ambulance Brigade demonstrates the fitting of civilian type respirators or gas masks. The weekly classes consisted of ten one-hour lectures, and 200 men responded to Poplar's call for volunteers.

Poplar Borough Council employees during training in gas decontamination work at Violet Road open-air swimming baths at the time of the crisis of 1938. Instructors were W.J. Rankin, left, and J.E. Spenser, right. Gas masks were issued to the general public at the end of September 1938. In Bethnal Green alone, 66,828 gas masks were distributed within two days.

Protecting Poplar Town Hall in Bow Road. Workmen are placing sandbags around the building, 1938. The Town Hall was built in 1935 to replace the building in Newby Place, Poplar.

These men are digging trenches in Poplar Recreation Ground during the crisis of 1938. Thousands of men were employed to dig trenches in parks around the East End, 875 in this park alone in September 1938. On 1 October the men were informed that their services were no longer required, and they were paid off.

Schoolchildren assembled at Devon's Road School, Bromley by Bow, getting ready for evacuation to Oxford at the outbreak of war in 1939. The children, wearing labels, are each equipped with a gas mask and haversack.

Children being evacuated at Finnis Street, Bethnal Green, 1939. The school was later demolished. Around one million children and 200,000 mothers were evacuated from London at the beginning of September 1939. Most drifted back to their homes when the threatened raids did not materialise. There were further evacuations in September 1940, and again in 1944 at the onset of the V1 attacks.

Children evacuated from Southern Grove School, Bow, seen happily posing for the cameraman at Wantage, Berkshire, 1939. This is one of the many pictures to publicise and promote evacuation.

Children from Columbia Market, Bethnal Green, on the lawn at Alwaton Hall, near Peterborough. Pictures like these were intended to reassure parents that their children were happy and being well taken care of following evacuation.

An ARP exercise in Calvert Avenue, Bethnal Green, 9 November 1939. A plane crash has been arranged, and the scene shows the 'German' airmen being arrested after leaping out of the plane. There was strong criticism of the performance of the Auxiliary Fire Service on a previous exercise in August 1939, when people enjoyed the spectacle of smoke bombs burning to indicate flaming buildings, but the fire engines took half an hour to reach the scene. Thirty-five fires were reported, but only thirty were supposed to have broken out!

Following on from the scene above, the plane has caught fire, and in the foreground 'casualties' wait to be attended to. These exercises were not always a complete success. Frank Lewey, Mayor of Stepney, notes in his book that during similar exercises in Stepney, things did not go to plan and one of the 'casualties', weary of lying on the pavement, left this note on his placard: 'Have bled to death and gone home.'

An ARP exercise in Poplar, 1939. Wardens take cover prior to the explosion of a bomb. Wardens were distinguished by a single stripe on their helmets, while deputy wardens had two.

The 'bomb' explodes on cue.

Brick surface shelters under construction in Streatfield Street, Stepney, 19 February 1940. These shelters were made available to families living in the adjacent houses, but were never very popular.

Trench shelters under construction in Limehouse Fields, 8 January 1940. Despite the rubble from the excavation work, a housewife has hung her washing on the line!

Sandbags for a temporary air raid shelter at Electric House, Bow Road, 1939. Electric House is on the north side of the road, on the corner of Alfred Street.

Children play on a surface air raid shelter, constructed of steel and sandbags. The photograph, by William Whiffin, featured in the local newspaper, the *East London Advertiser*, on 23 September 1938.

A closer look at the construction of a surface air raid shelter in Archibald Street, Bow, 1940. These shelters stood up remarkably well to blast damage.

Trench shelters under construction in the park in Tredegar Square, 15 March 1940. In the background can be seen the fine terraced houses on the north side of the Square.

The Blitz

People salvage their belongings after being bombed out of their homes in Lydia Street, off White Horse Lane, Stepney, September 1940. John Soul of 15 Lydia Street died following an air raid on Sunday 1 September 1940; Edith Buck was killed at no. 27, and Christina Collings of 22 Lydia Street was killed in Beaumont Square on 5 September 1940.

The Harvey family at 30 Surat Street, Bethnal Green, examine the results of the bombing on the night of 24/25 August 1940. These were the first bombs to fall on Bethnal Green. George Harvey is pointing to the spot where his daughter Agnes and her boyfriend Cyril were trapped in the house following the explosion. The other members of the family and the neighbours from no. 32 the Garners, were all in the Anderson shelter.

The Anderson shelter in the back yard at 30 Surat Street, Bethnal Green, 25 August 1940. Two bombs fell in the area, one directly on the Harveys' house, about 25 ft away from the shelter, the other in the park, behind the shelter. The location of the street was just to the north of Meath Gardens, parallel to Green Street, now Roman Road.

The East End ablaze during the Blitz, September 1940. On the right is the spire of St Matthias Church, on the south side of Poplar Recreation Ground, and in the lower foreground the East India Dock gate is just visible through the smoke, as is the chimney of Poplar Hospital. Many prominent buildings in the East India Dock Road were destroyed during the air raids that were to follow. William Whiffin's vantage point, on the north side of East India Dock Road, was possibly George Green's School. On 27 September 1939 Whiffin applied for a permit 'to take a series of photographs of happenings which may be of historical interest to the borough in time to come, including damage by aircraft (if any). . . . I quite understand these must not be exhibited or reproduced till better times.'

Another view of the fires caused by the devastating bombing in September 1940. William Whiffin, Poplar's most famous photographer, took this dramatic photograph of the East End, when fires raged in the docklands from the night of 7 September 1940. Whiffin was given a permit to take photographs of structural damage to buildings, with strict instructions that the location of the site should not be written at any time on the back of the print.

King George's Hall in East India Dock Road, showing the damage as a result of an air raid, 9 September 1940. The premises next door to the Hall, no. 166, Pearce Stanley's engineering works and garage, have been completely demolished, while H. Barnett, Overall Manufacturers, at no, 164, has fared no better.

Premises adjoining King George's Hall and the Poplar Methodist Church, in East India Dock Road. The motor engineering works and garage received a direct hit. Six people were killed and four injured here on 9 September 1940. Two days later the church was struck by an incendiary, and in 1943 it was severely damaged once more.

Devitt House in Wade's Place, Poplar, three days after it was severely damaged by a HE bomb on 13 October 1940. Frederick Reeder of 6 Devitt House and Thomas Strong of 36 Garford House received fatal injuries while two others were also injured. In the distance to the left can be seen Mallam Gardens houses, and beyond them the dome of the Queen Victoria Seamen's Rest is just visible. Devitt House was later rebuilt, and is part of the Will

Southill Street, Poplar, after the air raid on 24 September 1940 when a public shelter was hit. Emma Bearman, Helen and her children James, Charles and George Bearman were killed, along with Thomas and Emily Beard, Agnes Bingham, Sydney Foster and Elizabeth Hadley. Twenty-two others were injured. Southill Street connected Chrisp Street to Kerbey Street, and was parallel to Ricardo Street.

The Manor House, Brunswick Road, Poplar, stands derelict, March 1941. The house was built around the end of the 18th century. It was severely damaged during an air raid on Sunday 20 October 1940, and many of its fine wood carvings were destroyed. The Manor House was later demolished.

A lonely man contemplates the damage to a house at Wolverley Street, Bethnal Green, following an air raid on the night of 16/17 April 1941. This row of houses in a small turning off Bethnal Green Road was formerly weavers cottages. The houses were hit by a land mine at 3.25 am, causing extensive damage. The Wolverley Street School also suffered considerable damage from a HE bomb, and another bomb fell in the adjacent Canrobert Street at 3.40 am. ARP reports state that one person was killed and one injured during this incident.

The Falcon public house, Victoria Park Square, was demolished on 19/20 April 1941, when a 1000 kg bomb fell at the junction of Roman Road and Victoria Park Square. Charles Waghorn, aged 5, from East Greenwich, was injured in this incident; he died at Bethnal Green Hospital three days later. Morris Winger, Thomas Menote, and John Turner were killed in Victoria Park Square. The HE bomb caused severe damage to the Bethnal Green Estate and St John's Vicarage and set alight a bus which was completely gutted.

Benjamin Mason poses outside the air raid shelter, watched by two unnamed women, 1939. The shelter was at the rear of 8 Chaseley Street, Stepney. Living at no. 8 were Benjamin's father, also Benjamin, his mother Julia and sister Rachel. On Saturday 10 May 1941, Benjamin Mason Sr was injured in Chaseley Street; he died the next day in Mile End Hospital. Twenty-one others were killed in the Chaseley Street Shelter, which was in the Yorkshire Road railway arch at the end of the street. Among the dead was Elizabeth Hogg and her three daughters, Annie, Emily and Hilda.

Firemen tackling a blaze at Frank F. Scott, Shipping Brokers in Caroline Street, Ratcliff, 7 September 1941. The street was at the side of the Troxy cinema. Despite the severity of the fire, there is no sense of urgency here, and the trio on the right appear to have stopped for a gossip.

The Approach Tavern, Approach Road, Bethnal Green. This area was the target during several air raids, the worst in March and April 1941. On 19/20 April at 2.30 am a HE bomb landed in the road, causing a large crater and partially demolishing the pub. The landlord and his friends still manage to raise a toast to the cameraman!

City of London Chest Hospital, Approach Road, which received a direct hit on the night of 19/20 March 1941. The Chapel, the North Wing and the Nurses' Home were destroyed. The top wards had disappeared, and patients who had been moved into the basement for protection found themselves being sprayed with water as firemen fought to control the blaze. About a hundred patients were then moved into the nearby Parmiters School, using two ambulances in a shuttle service. The school had no windows and no electricity, and doctors and nurses worked through the night using hurricane lanterns. Only one patient was lost in this exercise.

Approach Road/Bishop's Way, 1941. On the night of 19/20 March, Charlotte and William Hedger of 48 Bishop's Way; Henry Swainsbury, William Franklin and Eliza Shacklady, all living in Approach Road, were among the casualties. An ARP report states that on that night a house in Approach Road was partially demolished trapping 18 people in the basement. The ferocity of the flames prevented any rescue attempt and they all perished. Several Sisters of Mercy living in Sewardstone Road also lost their lives that night.

Whitman House, on the Cornwall Estate, Bethnal Green, showing the effects of bomb damage following the air raid on 28 July 1941. Alan Homes, whose grandfather Henry Homes lived at 10 Whitman House, provided the following details: 'A bomb exploded in the courtyard to the east of the block, and the blast travelled down the alleyway, through the street door and into the bedroom of 2 Whitman House, killing William Allen, aged 19 years.' Following this there was a lull in enemy activity, and there were no further air raids until March 1943.

Arline Street, Bethnal Green, after an air raid which took place on the night of 10/11 May 1941. The clock tower of Columbia Market can be seen in the distance. The list of fatalities in this incident included Henry and Eliza Carter, and their daughter Kathleen, living at 13 Arline Street, William Hayes of 22 Arline Street and Albert Dowdell, who died next door at no. 23.

Columbia buildings, Bethnal Green: Search and Rescue in operation after an air raid on 10/11 May 1941. The public shelter on the right is covered with debris. Columbia Market itself, which contained a very large public shelter, was hit by a 50 kg bomb which entered the shelter through a ventilation shaft, killing a number of shelterers on Sunday 8 September 1940. Edward and Mary Birtwhistle and their son William of 65 Columbia Buildings, Maria and Daniel Barnard and their daughter Grace, Arthur and Florence Carter, Alice and George Desert, all of no. 52. Elizabeth and Percy Wells of no. 100 were also among the fatalities.

View of the destruction at the corner of Turin Street and Thorold Street, Bethnal Green, following the air raid on 16/17 April 1941. The photograph is taken from the first floor of Parker's newsagent shop, on the corner of St Matthew's Row. On the night of Wednesday 16 April five people were killed in Turin Street, James, Henry and Leslie Silvester at no. 1, Charles Swain at no. 5 and Firewatcher Albert Bennett of no. 9. Over 50 casualties were sustained in Thorold Street, with almost every house from nos 1 to 16 suffering fatalities, at no. 6 Clara Hamilton, her three daughters and two sons, at no. 8, five members of the Spicer family, and at no. 11, Margaret Burrell, her son and three daughters.

Dozens of ice cream barrows lie smashed under the rubble at Sugar Loaf Walk, Bethnal Green, 1941. The barrows belonged to Benjamin Rood, confectioner, of 279 Globe Road. On 11 January 1941 incendiaries caused fires in Sugar Loaf Walk, and the devastating air raid on 19/20 April 1941 completed the destruction.

Goodworth's Stores, 91–101 The Highway (north side), Stepney, was damaged during the air raid on 8 March 1941. Douglas Price, aged 18, who lived at 181 Downham Way, Lewisham, was killed in the building. Three firemen also lost their lives in the vicinity. They were Harry Greenberg, Charles King and Frederick Smith. This picture was taken a few days later on 14 March, when the fire brigade was still working at making the building safe. Goodworth's had a number of grocery outlets throughout London.

Braham Street, Whitechapel, seen from the corner of Plough Street and Buckle Street, 11 March 1941. Fireman Percy Millett of 48 Fuller Street, Bethnal Green, lost his life here on Sunday 8 September 1940.

Padstow House, damaged by bombs on Thursday 17 October 1940. The block consisted of seventy-nine flats, and was completed in March 1939. The caretaker, Mr H. Coates, gave a detailed account of the incident. At about 7.45 pm the siren went off and most of the flat tenants had gone into the underground shelter in the courtyard. Having checked that everyone was in the shelter, the warden left on his rounds. There was a sudden explosion, demolishing part of the building. While attempting to extinguish a fire which had started, he was suddenly aware that the shelter he had just left had collapsed, trapping the 170 people inside. Twenty-two injured were taken to hospital, but eight were unaccounted for. After several hours, Mrs Weddell, 80 years old, was brought out, but she died on her way to hospital. After several more hours of searching six more victims were brought out, dead. Finally, after seventeen hours, Mr Alexander was brought out, but died within minutes. On 19 March 1941, about fifty incendiary bombs were dropped on and around Padstow House and in May 1941, another bomb fell on the same shelter. Fortunately, by this time no one was in either the shelter or in Padstow House.

Rego's Garment Manufacturing Company on Bethnal Green Road was demolished in the air raid of 10/11 May 1941. Rego's was one of the largest employers of women in the East End rag trade.

The ruins of the Spotted Dog pub at 108 Poplar High Street. James Mann, aged 78, of 23 Bygrove Street, Elizabeth Percival, 78, and Rose Silence, 63, who lived at 110 Poplar High Street, were killed here during the air raid on 13 October 1940.

A workman surveys the damage at Clemence Street, Stepney, the result of the air raids on Sunday 8 September 1940, when Alfred Downing Williams, aged 60, of 37 Clemence Street, was killed. The picture is dated 2 July 1941.

Panoramic view of the Knott Street area, 11 March 1941. The photograph was taken from the roof of Searle House, and the view is northwards towards Mile End Road. In the background on the right is St Faith's Church. Shandy Street and Queen Mary and Westfield College and Mile End Hospital are just visible on the horizon. Knott Street was a small turning between Duckett Street and Ocean Street, Stepney. The Commercial Gas Company in the adjacent Harford Street was a prime target.

Hanbury Street by Spital Street: view of the bomb damage following an air raid on 10 September 1940. This picture was taken on 29 September. Despite the total destruction of the building on the left, the street shelter has survived the blast and remains intact.

Commercial Road, near Adler Street, Stepney, 2 May 1941. Workmen are attempting to repair the 48-inch gas mains, which have been exposed as the result of high explosive bombs. The air raid on the night of 16 April was particularly bad for Commercial Road; fatalities were heavy and included several ARP personnel.

Commercial Road, on the corner with Adler Street, 9 May 1941. The Road Repair Parties led by the Divisional Surveyor Edward Moule carried on their relentless task of repairing the craters formed by the bombs, which not only destroyed the road surface, but the mains and sewers below. Their first task was to rope off the craters and place red lamps around 'to prevent vehicles and pedestrians falling into same'.

Damage to J. Scott's Bakery, 55 Hartley Street, Bethnal Green, 1941. The bakery was on the corner of Kirkwall Place. The two young children seem quite unconcerned by the activities of the three men among the debris.

A young man surveys the damage to Scott's Bakery, Bethnal Green, viewed from Brierly Street. The street was fairly small and connected Royston Street to Hartley Street. The baker's van is just visible under the rubble.

The Auxiliary Services

Mr W. Roberts, Fire Precautions Officer, 'B' Division, Poplar, and formerly warden at Post B132, gives the Victory sign. Mr Roberts was specially commended for his bravery.

London's War Weapons Week, 17–24 May 1939. A Bethnal Green Civil Defence lorry, specially decorated with flags and posters urging people to invest in National Savings, with slogans, 'We can't lose if we lend,' and 'Britain's worth saving'. The lorry is passing Bethnal Green Gardens, along Cambridge Heath Road.

Civil Defence March Past in Wilmot Street, Bethnal Green, *c.* 1939. When first formed, the Home Guard were provided with armbands and a few archaic weapons, and drilled with broom handles and even ancient pike staffs. They were later equipped with khaki battledress, steel helmets, and .300 Springfield rifles with bayonet, which were obsolete weapons, courtesy of the American army. At its peak the Home Guard consisted of over one and a half million armed men.

Bethnal Green Town Hall Home Guard march past Bethnal Green Gardens, Cambridge Heath Road, *c.* 1939.
All three boroughs carried out vigorous campaigns to recruit volunteers into their Civil Defence services.

A Local Defence Volunteer unit consisting of Poplar Borough Council employees, formed in June 1940 for the
protection of the Town Hall and Council Offices at night. It was later absorbed into the Home Guard.

81

First aid workers, at Poplar Baths, East India Dock Road, Poplar, *c.* 1939. The young woman seated on the left appears to be on familiar terms with the young man standing behind her! Although there is another photograph of the same young man striking a comic pose, he is as yet unidentified.

Chief Warden Smith of Poplar directing his wardens George Freshwater and Sam Turton, 29 October 1942. Casualties among ARP wardens and firefighters were high and accounted for a large percentage of the total fatalities in the East End.

Full-time women wardens outside Bromley Public Hall, Bow Road, 15 October 1941. Among the ladies in the picture are Mrs O'Leary, Mrs Lakey, Mrs Stewart, Mrs Watson and Mrs Margetts.

An unknown woman ARP Warden, Poplar area. The hat and overall were dark blue, the badge on the hat and buttons were silver. The photograph was taken by Griffiths photographers, of 98 Armagh Road, Old Ford.

Heavy Rescue squad in action after the raid on 27/28 July 1941. Several bombs were dropped in the vicinity of Hill Place Street, Latham Street, Arcadia Street and Broomfield Street, and some 53 people were killed and 79 injured. At 2.30 am the shelter in the old Royal National Lifeboat Institution in Broomfield Street was hit with a high explosive bomb, killing 34 people. Five complete families were wiped out and many more injured. Among the dead were John and Victoria Mitchell and their five children.

Heavy Rescue party endeavouring to reach trapped shelterers at the Co-operative Wholesale Society's store, Hill Place Street, Poplar, following an air raid on 27/28 July 1941. Dr Haydon Jones, a local GP, is seen still wearing his pyjama jacket.

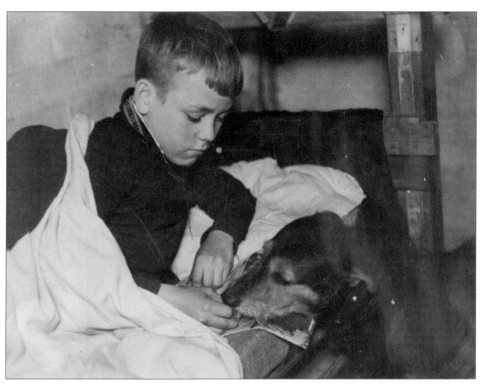

Rip offers comfort to a youngster in an air raid shelter, and is rewarded with a titbit especially saved for him. Rip was found by Warden E. King of Post B132, Southill Street, Poplar. King took care of him and he became an 'official' ARP dog, helping the squad search for people buried under debris. He proved to be an invaluable asset in their work and was awarded the Dickin Medal, the animals' VC, 'for locating many air-raid victims buried by rubble during the blitz of 1940'. One of those he helped to find was Mrs King, who was trapped for four hours beneath their bombed home, sustaining a fracture.

A scene of devastation in Hill Place Street, Poplar, following an air raid on 11/12 September 1940. The water-filled bomb crater was caused by a parachute mine. ARP workers from Post B132 are seen removing a body from the scene. Henry and Emma Marshall of 28 Lindfield Street were killed in this raid. In the background street shelter no. 184 has survived relatively unscathed. On 7 September 1940 in nearby Lindfield Street, twenty casualties were reported under the wreckage of a building. Among the dead were Dorothy and Beatrice Taylor, Elizabeth Ford and Winifred Newman, all at 29 Lindfield Street.

The Destruction Continues – Nothing is Spared

Victoria Park Congregational Church, Approach Road, in ruins. The photograph is undated, but the area around Approach Road and St James's Avenue adjacent to Victoria Park suffered very heavy bombardment on 19 March and 19/20 April 1941.

The Jewish Synagogue at the Shoreditch end of Bethnal Green Road lies in ruins after an incident on 10/11 May 1941.

Clearing up in the Jews' Burial Ground, Mile End Road, following an air raid. The Burial Ground is now within Queen Mary and Westfield College grounds.

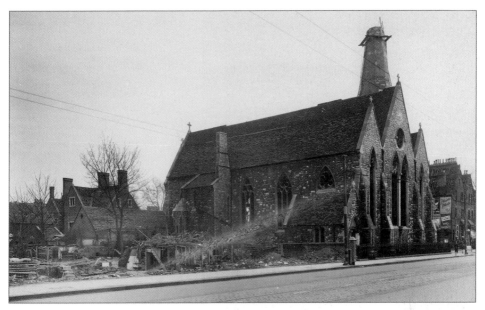

St Paul's Church, on the corner of Burdett Road and St Paul's Way. The spire had suffered damage and had to be removed. Later on 29 July 1944, during a particularly heavy night of bombing, the church was completely destroyed when the spire, acting as a chimney, drew up the flames and the massive timbers in the church burned furiously.

St Paul's Way, looking east to the junction of Bow Common Lane, showing the destruction in Selsey Street, 1941. The spire of Holy Name Church is in the background. Rose Stovell of 1 Selsey Street, Mary Lane of no. 37 and Albert Blake all died here on 7 September 1940.

Bethnal Green Library opened a branch library in the Bethnal Green Tube shelter, with a selection of 4,000 books. The first of its kind, the library which was only 15 ft square, served the public from 21 October 1941 until 6 February 1942, when it was closed.

St George's Library, Cable Street, in ruins, 18 November 1941. The library building was destroyed in an incident on 10/11 May 1941. Mr J. Conolly, the District Warden, reported that this was the worst night he could remember, when Stepney received a 'terrific shower of explosives and incendiaries'.
Dr Hannah Billig, a local GP, lived a few doors away at 198 Cable Street. She attended many of the shelters on her rounds in Wapping, and was called to the Orient Wharf Shelter, Wapping, on 13 March 1941, where despite being injured herself, she continued to attend to the casualties. She was awarded the George Medal for her bravery.

Mile End Hospital, Bancroft Road, Stepney, showing the destruction from a V1 rocket on 6 July 1944. Heavy casualties were inflicted on Bancroft Road and Moody Street on Friday 28 July 1944.

A view of the partially destroyed Mile End Hospital, Bancroft Road, Stepney, following the V1 rocket attack in July 1944.

The air raid shelter at the London Hospital, Whitechapel Road, 13 April 1940. The sign to the right says: 'The London Hospital is in great need of your help.'

London Hospital Nurses' Quarters, 1941, showing the effects of bomb blast. On Monday 23 September 1941 the King and Queen visited the London Hospital and talked to air raid victims in four wards there. The royal family made frequent visits to the East End of London during the Blitz and later. They were acutely conscious of the suffering endured by the ordinary people, and when Buckingham Palace was bombed, the Queen famously remarked: 'Now we can look the East End in the face.'

St George's Hospital was destroyed in an air raid on 11 March 1941. The hospital was situated towards the end of Wapping Lane.

St Peter's Church, Wapping, 1941. The church was badly damaged, but it fared better than St John's Church, the parish church of Wapping, nearby, which was destroyed, leaving only the bell tower. St Peter's was restored in 1956, and is now St Peter's with St John's. Sister Catherine (Coates), of the Sisters of Charity was killed in an air raid on 15 October 1940 at St Peter's Mission House.

St Simon Zelotes Church, Morpeth Street, on the corner of Knottisford Street, destroyed by a high explosive bomb on 21 October 1943. A group of bystanders watch with interest as the Rescue team sift through the rubble of the store opposite the church.

The War Effort – Coping with Crisis

Her Majesty Queen Elizabeth walking down St Peter's Avenue, 17 June 1943. Councilor Sanders is talking to the Queen, who is accompanied by the Mayor and Mayoress, the Town Clerk and Councillor Tate. The Queen was keenly aware of the hardship endured by people in the Blitz, and sent furniture, linen, carpets and rugs, as well as prams for distribution among those who had lost everything.

Display of official notices advertising salvage collection, at the entrance to Poplar Town Hall, 1941. Poplar went on an all-out offensive on the collection of waste paper and metal, resulting in a huge stockpile at Northumberland Wharf.

A vast collection of salvaged articles, from shoes to saucepans and bathtubs, was accumulated at Northumberland Wharf. Sadly much of this salvage, so enthusiastically handed over for the war effort, was unsuitable for recycling and ended up being dumped in the sea.

The Victoria Wine Company's shop displays a novel way of protecting the plate-glass window, with a decoration of a church made from gummed paper, 1942. The poster on the left states: 'You have to be prepared, so why not join our Christmas Club.' The shop was in East India Dock Road, Poplar.

Poplar's salvage drive. Vehicle no. 39 of the Poplar Borough Council in Paton Close, Bow, with posters urging people to bring out their books for salvage, during London Book Recovery and Salvage Drive, 1943. Posters have slogans such as, 'The nation needs your books for the services and for salvage.' 'Books for the forces, bombed libraries and munitions of war.' 'Rags for salvage will give the troops more blankets.'

Members of the Services, the RAF, Civil Defence and nurses gather round at the Memorial Service held on the site of Single Street School, on 15 September 1942, the second anniversary of the Battle of Britain. The street and the site of the school have become part of Mile End Park.

The bombed shell of Single Street School, near Canal Street, Stepney, was chosen as the East End site to commemorate the victory of the Battle of Britain. The Rector and Rural Dean of Stepney, the Rev. R. French, conducted the Service on 15 September 1942. On display are the flags of the allied countries.

Winston Churchill visits the East End. His first visit took place on 8 September 1940, with his brother Jack, his son-in-law Duncan Sandys and his Chief of Staff, General Ismay. One of the first places they visited was the Peabody Buildings in John Fisher Street, Stepney, where more than forty people were killed and many more injured when the surface air raid shelter received a direct hit the previous night. Ismay recalled that when Churchill got out of his car he was greeted with cries of 'It was good of you to come Winnie. We thought you'd come. We can take it. Give it 'em back.' Churchill was so overcome with emotion he broke down and wept. The tour of the East End lasted all afternoon and into the late evening, by which time the Luftwaffe had returned to resume their bombing.

Mrs Eleanor Roosevelt, wife of the President of the United States, pays a visit to the Tilbury Shelter with King George VI, October 1942. Another visitor to the same shelter was Lady Edwina Mountbatten, then deputy Superintendent-in-Chief of the St John Ambulance Brigade. She found thousands of shelterers occupying every inch of space, trying to sleep on old crates, on deckchairs, and on the wooden floor, which was awash with urine and piled with excrement. There were just two buckets designated as lavatories. Lady Mountbatten took immediate steps to remedy the appalling situation.

Doris and Elsie Waters, famous radio entertainers, who played the popular characters, Gert and Daisy, serve tea at the mobile canteen they presented to Poplar in October 1941. The Waters family lived at Rounton Road, Bow. Their famous brother Horace John Waters changed his name to Jack Warner and found fame later as Dixon of Dock Green.

Elsie and Doris Waters unveil the mobile canteen which was presented by them, their family, friends and audiences, to the Borough of Poplar in October 1941. Elsie and Doris are removing the flag, watched by the Mayor and Mayoress, Alderman A.W. and Mrs Overland.

The display for Stepney Warship Week, 21–28 March, goes up on 13 March 1942. The campaign was formally opened by Mr C.R. Attlee, MP for Limehouse and Deputy Prime Minister, on Saturday 21 March at the People's Palace, which had become Stepney's temporary Town Hall. The target for HMS *Rocket* was set at £750,000. The slogan adopted was 'Out of the Pocket into the Rocket'.

Bethnal Green Warship Week, 1942. Bethnal Green Borough Council held a week-long campaign using posters and hoardings to urge people to donate generously to the scheme. The borough adopted the 1,490-ton frigate HMS *Crane*, which was launched on 9 November 1942 and completed on 10 May 1943. The borough continued to maintain a close relationship with the ship, and following its scrapping in the early 1960s the Admiralty presented Bethnal Green with the ship's bell. The bell is now on display in Tower Hamlets Town Hall, Mulberry Place.

Men playing cards in the Poplar Methodist Mission air raid shelter. The shelter was in the boiler house of the Mission, and seen here are Mr Walker, Rev. I. Morgan, Mrs Walker, Mr W. Carey and Mr J. Pearce. The church, known as Lax's Church, stood in East India Dock Road, by Poplar Recreation Ground. It was severely damaged during an air raid on 11 September 1940 and again in 1943. It was later demolished.

The Bee-Gees Concert Party at the Bethnal Green Town Hall, Patriot Square, helping to raise funds during Bethnal Green's Warship Week, 21–28 March 1942. The fund-raising was a great success, and Bethnal Green adopted the 1,490-ton frigate HMS *Crane*.

Sewardstone Road Farm, May 1943. The sign on the side of the cart reads: 'Bethnal Green Bomb Sites Association'. The gardens on bombed sites idea was the initiative of Sir Wyndham Deedes, Chief Warden of Bethnal Green. Sir Wyndham Henry Deedes lived at Temple House, 17 Victoria Park Square, from 1923 to 1939, after a distinguished career in the army intelligence service in Cairo and Palestine. He retired to Bethnal Green and served on Bethnal Green Council and the London County Council. In 1939 he moved to nearby St Margaret's in Old Ford Road.

Mr W.J. Jordan, High Commissioner for New Zealand, at the opening of the Russia Lane garden, Bethnal Green, May 1942. Children and adults were encouraged to create their own allotments on bomb-damaged sites, growing vegetables, such as peas, potatoes and cabbages, and keeping rabbits. They borrowed spades and shovels from the local fire brigade.

The War Goes On –
With Tragic Consequences

Bethnal Green Underground converted for use as an air raid shelter. The station was under construction from Liverpool Street to Loughton, but because of the worsening conditions, work stopped on 24 May 1940. The council then converted it into a shelter in October 1941, with bunks for 5,000 people and extra space for another 5,000 if needed.

A view of the platform at Bethnal Green Underground station. Initially, the government tried to prevent the use of the underground stations as shelters, as it was feared that people terrified by raids would refuse to come back to the surface, a hypothetical state of mind known as deep shelter mentality. Londoners' response to this was to buy a ticket just before a raid was anticipated and stay down. As this practice became more widespread, the government changed its policy. Tube stations in daily use were organised as shelters in the evenings, and incomplete stations, such as Bethnal Green, were opened up and furnished with bunks and toilets.

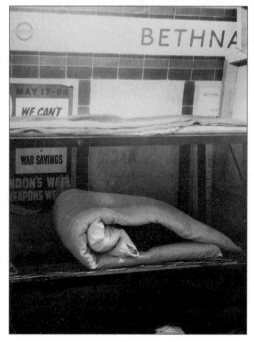

Bunks at Bethnal Green Underground station platform. With thousands of people sheltering in the tube station every night even more bunks had to be erected on the platform. Owing to a shortage of male workers and the urgency of getting these bunks in place, the Boy Scouts were asked to volunteer for the work. People would not normally leave their bedding unattended, as even those asleep in the shelters would find their blankets stolen from around them.

Entrance to the Bethnal Green Tube station, scene of the worst civilian disaster on 3 March 1943. This picture was taken shortly afterwards. When the shelter was opened in October 1941, about 5,000 people used it every night. The numbers later dropped to hundreds. On 1 and 2 March the numbers were 587 and 850 respectively. On the evening of Wednesday 3 March, between 500 and 600 were already in the shelter, but by 8.17 pm another 1,000 were making their way down the stairway. Ten minutes later a salvo of rockets from the newly installed gun battery in Victoria Park, approximately half a mile away, caused panic, and it was immediately thought that another air raid had begun. About 200 people around the entrance to the shelter surged forward, pushing their way down the stairs. A witness on the landing below, and two others, saw a woman, holding a child and a bundle, stumble near the foot of the flight of 19 steps; an elderly man behind her also fell. Those coming in from the street continued to press down the steps, so that within a minute there were hundreds of people crushed together, lying on top of one another. Within ninety seconds, 173 people were dead, 62 of them children. The woman who tripped was found alive, her baby dead. Later examination was to show that the sole cause of death was suffocation, with only one broken bone. Survivors, 60 needing hospital treatment, suffered bruising, shock and minor injuries. It took the Civil Defence and the police over three hours to clear all the casualties. Of the 173 killed, only 51 were registered for bunks in the shelter, while another 30 were known users. The rest were using the place for the first time.

Workmen fixing handrails at the entrance to the Bethnal Green Tube shelter shortly after the tragic incident on 3 March 1943. The shelter had only one entrance, with an emergency exit half a mile away in another borough. There were no handrails, no crush barrier, no white lines, and it was lit by a single 25 watt bulb. From the entrance there were 19 steps down to a landing, measuring 15 ft by 12 ft. A right-hand turn followed by 7 more steps led into the ticket hall. Visitors to Bethnal Green station today still use the same stairway which, except for the addition of handrails at the side and centre of the stairs, remains the same. A plaque has been placed above the entrance commemorating the incident, the largest civilian accident recorded during the war, which accounted for a third of all wartime deaths in Bethnal Green. Possibly the worst aspect of this incident was that no bombs fell anywhere on the district that night.

Tackling a blaze somewhere in Poplar. ARP wardens and firefighters risked their lives on innumerable occasions. One incident, not reported at the time because of censorship, occurred on the night of Saturday 19 April 1941 – the occasion of some of the heaviest bombing raids on London and the East End with over 1026 tons of high explosives and 153,096 incendiaries dropped. It was also the night of one of the worst tragedies suffered by the Fire Brigade. Old Palace School, St Leonard's Street, Bromley by Bow, was being used as a sub-station for the London Fire Brigade and as the HQ of the local Rescue Services. Local fire stations were pressed to their limits and four auxiliary fire service crews and their pumps from Beckenham were directed to Old Palace School to reinforce those already hard at work. just after midnight. At 1.30 am with other local crews they were mustering for orders. At 1.53 am the school received a direct hit and one part was completely demolished while a major fire started throughout what was left. Thirty-six firemen were killed, including all four of the Beckenham crews.

The scene of the devastation caused by the first V1 flying bomb, which fell on a railway bridge in Grove Road, Bethnal Green, at 4.25 am on 13 June 1944. Six people living in Grove Road were killed, including Helen Woodcraft, 19, and her son Thomas, aged 8 months, of no. 64. The other nearby residents were Dora Cohen, Constance Day, William Rogers and Leonard Sherman, aged 12. Seen in the centre of the picture carrying a shovel on his shoulder is Henry Homes, from Portman Place Heavy Rescue Squad. He lived at 10 Whitman Place, scene of an earlier incident. Rumours ran rife as to what this new weapon was, but the government refused to divulge any details. Two days later, on Thursday 15 June, 74 flying bombs landed in the London area, and the government revealed that this was a new type of weapon, a pilotless aircraft. It became known as a doodlebug or buzzbomb. The last V1 attack was on 1 September – and waiting in the wings was the next weapon, the V2 long-range rocket.

Hughes Mansions, Vallance Road, Stepney, 9 April 1945. On 27 March 1945 at approximately 7.25 am a V2 rocket struck the middle block of flats, wrecking 60 of the 93 flats, and inflicting a heavy loss of life. The V2 long-range rocket was 45 ft long, weighed 14 tons, with a one ton warhead, and travelled faster than the speed of sound. Launched from mobile platforms in The Hague, they were very difficult to detect. The King and Queen visited the scene during their tour on 9 May 1945.

Hughes Mansions, Stepney. This block of flats was farthest from Vallance Road and was completely destroyed by the last V2 rocket to fall on London, on 27 March 1945. It is a scene of utter desolation. Rescue crews worked through the night recovering bodies, some of which were found on the roof of the adjacent St Peter's Hospital. The final toll was 134 dead, 48 injured. The majority of the casualties were Jewish families, and in some instances an entire family was killed. Miriam Moses, the warden at Brady Girls' Club, was among those who assisted in the rescue. Renee Oliver, who lived in an adjacent block, recalls a lonely man wandering around the ruins at night for weeks calling for Annie. Was he looking for Annie Freedman, who went out to buy a loaf of bread for breakfast, and never returned?

King George VI and Queen Elizabeth on a visit to the East India Dock Road, accompanied by the Princesses Elizabeth and Margaret, Wednesday 9 May 1945, when the royal family toured bomb sites in the East End. They are standing near the site of the Eagle public house, which was demolished, along with a nursing home for sisters, by a V2 rocket on 7 March, at 11.50 am, killing 20 people and injuring a further 120. Many of the victims had been standing at the bus stop outside All Saints Church. Rescue work went on for 36 hours non-stop, and dogs were used to search for people under the wreckage. The Queen chats to the Mayor of Poplar, Mrs Sadler, while the King talks to Mr H.E. Smith, Chief Warden, and Mr S.A. Hamilton, the Deputy Town Clerk.

A Cause for
Celebration

The Memorial Window in Bethnal Green Library, restored, following its damage by enemy action on 1 September 1940. The window is on the first floor of the Library. The refurbished window was unveiled by the Mayor Councillor A.G. Clarke, and re-dedicated by the Rev. A.A. Gorbold on Remembrance Sunday, 12 November 1950.

March Past of Poplar Wardens, Sunday 10 June 1945. The farewell parade of the Civil Defence and allied services, when King George VI, accompanied by Queen Elizabeth and Princess Elizabeth, the present Queen, took the salute in Hyde Park.

King George VI and Queen Elizabeth talk to Stepney wardens on Wednesday 9 May 1945, during the royal family's tour of the East End's bomb sites. When they stopped at Hughes Mansions in Vallance Road, Stepney, the large crowd that turned out to see them sang the National Anthem.

A street party held outside 74 Quilter Street on the Jesus Hospital Estate, Bethnal Green, 1945, one of the dozens held in the East End to celebrate the end of six long years of war. On 19 March 1941 an unexploded 250 kg bomb buried itself in the centre of the carriageway. Everyone poses happily for the camera, but a closer look at the table reveals the sandwiches are already beginning to curl! (A street party was held on Saturday 6 October in Quilter Street, with tea at the Friends' Hall, Barnet Grove, but it is uncertain if this is the same one.)

Victory party held at Leyland House in Hale Street, Poplar, Friday 25 May 1945. The decorations at these parties are more restrained than those of the First World War. On the same day a German U-boat was put on public display in the Western Dock, London Docks, close to Tower Bridge, and 20,000 people queued up to have a look inside it.

A young sailor, Ernest Bickley, of Poplar, 18 February 1944.

Vera Aulford, serving her country, 1944. She was a member of St Matthias Church, Poplar.

Loris Carrington, member of St Matthias Church, Poplar. The caption on the reverse of the photo says 'Our little stokehole maid during the Blitz 1939–1940, Poplar.'

A dashing young soldier, L.S. Northwood, with his beret at an impossible angle, poses for the camera on 9 April 1945.

Children gather at Bethnal Green Town Hall to receive their gift parcels from the Mayor, Councillor G.R.H. Hemsley, 24 February 1949. The parcels were sent from Canada, and members of the Women's Voluntary Services helped to distribute them to over 400 children.

Sabbarton Street, Poplar: young girls take a stroll through a bomb site, 18 January 1949. In the far distance can be seen the spire of All Saints Church.

Temporary homes in Stepney, in the vicinity of St Dunstan's Church. Prefabricated buildings like these became a familiar sight all around the East End, and although they were described as ten year houses, the inference being that they would be replaced within that time, a few were still in existence in the 1990s.

Arcadia Street, Poplar, 1949. Four years on, Poplar houses still lie in ruins, but temporary housing can be seen in the centre of the picture. Poplar retained many of its prefabs well into the 1980s, and the last were demolished in the mid-1990s.

Gosling House, Sutton Street, Stepney, 17 August 1943. The building was severely damaged during an air raid in 1941. It was built in 1936 to house tenants from the Beccles Street Slum Clearance areas.

Gosling House following repair and refurbishment, *c.* 1950. These pictures present an excellent 'before and after' view.

Giant crane at the corner of Upper North Street and East India Dock Road, 1951. The crane marked the site of the Architecture, Town Planning and Building Research Exhibition in Poplar. It was 200 ft high and was the tallest crane ever to be made in Britain.

A view of the Festival of Britain Exhibition site on the Lansbury Estate in Poplar, 1951. This area of the East End which lies alongside the East India Dock Road was selected for the live architecture section of the Festival of Britain. Low rise blocks were designed by various architects and the aim was to design and build postwar housing that would be models for the future.

Acknowledgements

Alfieri Picture Service
BBC
East London Advertiser
Fox Photos
Mrs Grace Gibson
A.P. Griffiths
The Trustees of the Imperial War Museum
Illustrated London News
Mr D. Jones
London News Agency Photos Ltd
Philip Mernick
Marx Memorial Library
Paul Mancrieff
New York Times
PLA Monthly
Poplar Methodist Mission

Planet News Ltd
Mr A.S. Ramsey
Sport and General Press Agency
S and G Press Agency Ltd
Tower Hamlets Local History Library and
    Archives
John Topham
Mr W. Turner
The Topical Press Agency Ltd
William Whiffin
Andy Wood, LBTH Photographer
C.I.P. Webb
Mr A. White
Mr F. Wilkinson
Mr J. Waters

The Rivoli cinema, Whitechapel Road, which opened in 1921. It was destroyed during the Second World War and the façade of the cinema stood in Whitechapel Road for twenty years before being demolished. The remains of the cinema are shown as it appeared in November 1961. The Citroën garage now occupies part of the site, while the East London Mosque (1985) was built on the remaining land.